THE C
AND REC

REBELLION A

SLAVE STATES, FREE STATES, AND THE MISSOURI COMPROMISE

COMPILED BY JOANNE RANDOLPH

★

PowerKiDS
press

Published in 2018 by The Rosen Publishing Group, Inc.
29 East 21st Street, New York, NY 10010

"A Balancing Act: The Missouri Compromise" by Phyllis Raybin Emert from Cobblestone
Magazine (January 2002).
"A Nation Divided" by Craig E. Blohm from Cobblestone Magazine (January 2001).

Cataloging-in-Publication Data

Names: Randolph, Joanne.
Title: Slave states, free states, and the Missouri Compromise / compiled by Joanne Randolph.
Description: New York : PowerKids Press, 2018. | Series: The Civil War and Reconstruction:
rebellion and rebuilding | Includes glossary and index.
Identifiers: LCCN ISBN 9781538341025 (pbk.) | ISBN 9781538341018 (library bound) |
ISBN 9781538341032 (6 pack)
Subjects: LCSH: Missouri compromise--Juvenile literature. | Slavery--United States--History--
Juvenile literature. | United States--Politics and government--1815-1861--Juvenile literature.
Classification: LCC E373.S538 2018 | DDC 973.5'4--dc23

Designer: Katelyn E. Reynolds
Editor: Joanne Randolph

Photo credits: Cvr, p. 1 Interim Archives/Getty Images; cvr, pp. 1–32 (background texture)
javarman/Shutterstock.com; cvr, pp. 1–32 (flags) cybrain/Shutterstock.com; cvr, pp. 1–32
(scroll) Seregam/Shutterstock.com; pp. 5, 20, 23 Tintazul: Júlio Reis/derivative work: JWB
(talk)/Wikipedia.org; pp. 6 , 10, 15, 21, 25, 28 (both) courtesy of the Library of Congress;
p. 8 Hulton Archive/Getty Images; p. 13 National Archives and Records Administration,
cataloged under the National Archives Identifier (NAID) 528293 (https://catalog.archives.
gov/id/528293)/Wikipedia.org; p. 17 Google Art Project/National Portrait Gallery,
Washington/Wikipedia.org; p. 19 Prisma/UIG via Getty Images; p. 27 U.S. National
Archives & Records Administration.

Manufactured in the United States of America

CONTENTS

WORDS IN THE GLOSSARY APPEAR
IN **BOLD** TYPE THE FIRST TIME
THEY ARE USED IN THE TEXT.

★

THE MISSOURI COMPROMISE OF 1820

Tensions were running high in the United States during the 1800s over the issue of slavery, among other political and economic issues. One of the final **compromises** that tried to keep the peace was the Compromise of 1850. It made concessions to Southern states that wanted to allow slavery in new states and territories. It also made concessions to the North, which wanted slavery to be banned from all new states and territories. It didn't solve the underlying issues, but it probably put off the Civil War for another decade.

To better understand the Compromise of 1850, it is helpful to go back thirty years prior to it and study another compromise. The Missouri Compromise of 1820 raised issues about the balance of power in Congress and the power of the federal government to establish rules for and restrictions on the individual states. But perhaps most important, the 1820 compromise vote revealed **sectional** views.

It was becoming clear that strong opposing positions on slavery were beginning to take root. There were three parts to the Missouri Compromise. First, Maine was admitted to the Union as a free state. Second, Missouri was admitted as a slave state. And third, slavery was forbidden in lands acquired in the Louisiana Purchase of 1803 north of latitude 36 degrees, 30 minutes (with the exception of Missouri).

FREE STATES AND TERRITORIES

SLAVE STATES AND TERRITORIES

CLOSED TO SLAVERY BY MISSOURI COMPROMISE OF 1820

OPEN TO SLAVERY BY MISSOURI COMPROMISE OF 1820

MISSOURI COMPROMISE LINE

THE PRIMARY AIM OF
THE MISSOURI COMPROMISE OF 1820
WAS TO PRESERVE THE BALANCE OF POWER
BETWEEN FREE AND SLAVE STATES.

★

This image depicts slaves picking cotton on a Georgia plantation.

By 1820, every Northern state either had **prohibited** slavery or provided for its gradual **abolition**. The South, meanwhile, had become increasingly dependent on the labor of slaves and the slave trade.

With the South relying on slavery to keep its **plantation economy** going, Southerners resented Northern interference in Southern business. In addition to sectional differences regarding slavery, many Southerners believed that legislation passed by Congress favored Northern industry at the expense of Southern agriculture.

When the Missouri **Territory** applied for statehood in 1819, a balance of power existed in the Senate. There were 11 free states and 11 slave states, each represented by 22 senators. If Missouri — with its ten thousand slaves, representing about sixteen percent of the area's population — was admitted to the Union as a slave state, this balance would be upset.

Representative James Tallmadge Jr. of New York was concerned by the advantage the South had in the **Electoral College**. (Slaves counted as three-fifths of a person for voting purposes, although they themselves could not vote.) He also worried about the need to set a careful **precedent**, since Missouri was the first state to be carved out of the Louisiana Purchase.

Tallmadge added an amendment with two parts to the bill for Missouri's admission to the Union. In addition to prohibiting the entry of additional slaves into Missouri, the amendment stated that "all children of slaves, born within the said state, after the admission thereof into the Union, shall be free, but may be held to service until the age of twenty-five years."

In effect, Tallmadge's addition provided for a gradual abolition of slavery in Missouri. This worried the South. Southerners opposed the power of Congress to set conditions on the admission of a state into the Union and believed the restrictions would affect the equality among all the states. The debate that followed was long and loud.

THOMAS JEFFERSON SERVED AS THE NATION'S THIRD PRESIDENT. THOUGH HE WORKED TO GRADUALLY END THE INSTITUTION OF SLAVERY, HE OWNED HUNDREDS OF SLAVES.

No action was taken until the next session of Congress, in which Maine applied for admission to the Union as a state. Here was an opportunity for compromise. Maine was admitted to statehood on March 15, 1820, as a free state, while Missouri was authorized to form a constitution and state government that supported slavery. The Arkansas Territory also would be open to slavery, but the rest of the Louisiana Purchase lands (north of the 36 degrees, 30 minutes latitude line) would be closed to slavery.

Former president Thomas Jefferson, a Southerner from Virginia, believed the Missouri Compromise deepened the hostility between the North and the South: "But this momentous question [the Missouri Compromise] like a firebell in the night awakened and filled me with terror. I considered it the **knell** of the Union." He feared the country would become permanently divided along sectional lines. He died in 1826 and was spared the sorrow of seeing his worst fears realized.

The Missouri Compromise was important because it revealed basic sectional differences: the South's strong commitment to slavery and the North's equally vigorous opposition. Historian Glover Moore called the Missouri Compromise the first "full-scale dress rehearsal" for the "great sectional contest" that was to come in the 1850s.

ANOTHER VIEW ON THE MISSOURI COMPROMISE: A NATION DIVIDED

In February 1861, Jefferson Davis was tending his garden with his wife, Varina, when he looked up to see a lone rider galloping at full speed toward the Davis plantation, Brierfield. Reining his horse to a quick stop, the rider leaned over and handed Davis a telegram.

"Sir: We are directed to inform you that you are this day unanimously elected President of the Provisional Government of the Confederate States of America and to request you to come to Montgomery immediately."

It was an honor, but one that Davis had not sought. An experienced soldier, he would rather have commanded the Confederate army. But Davis felt it was his duty to accept this responsibility.

JEFFERSON DAVIS, SHOWN HERE, SERVED AS PRESIDENT OF THE CONFEDERATE STATES OF AMERICA FROM 1861 TO 1865 DURING THE AMERICAN CIVIL WAR.

★

THE ROAD TO THE CIVIL WAR

Sadly, what was one nation, **indivisible**, soon would become two nations divided. Yet, in many ways, that split already existed and had for more than two hundred years. The first Africans landed on North American shores in August 1619. Twenty African **indentured** servants were delivered to the Jamestown (Virginia) colony.

As the early colonies grew and plantations spread, a permanent workforce was needed to do the backbreaking work in tobacco, rice, and cotton fields. The North, with smaller farms and more industrial growth, had little need for slaves. Thus, as America grew, an invisible line developed between northern and southern ways of life.

In 1819, the territory of Missouri wanted to join the United States as a slaveholding state. At the time, there was an equal number of senators from northern (free) and southern (slave) states. Admitting a new slave state would tip the balance in the Senate in favor of slavery. In March 1820, the Senate reached what is called the Missouri Compromise: Missouri would enter the Union as a slaveholding state, while Maine would join as a free state. The agreement maintained the delicate balance between slave and free states. It also created a line that extended westward from Missouri's southern border, above which all new states would be free.

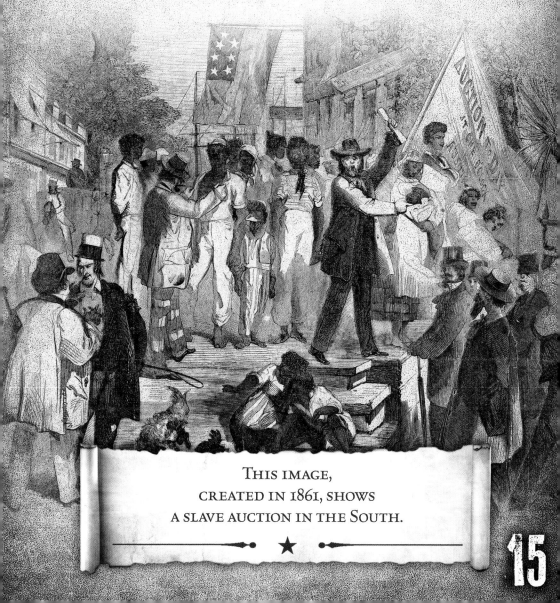

THIS IMAGE, CREATED IN 1861, SHOWS A SLAVE AUCTION IN THE SOUTH.

IMPORT TARIFFS

By the 1830s, the United States, led by the industrial North, had imposed a series of **tariffs** on imported merchandise. These tariffs, or taxes, made it more expensive for Americans to buy European-manufactured goods. But the less Americans bought from abroad, the fewer raw materials European manufacturers would purchase from southern plantations. Vice President John C. Calhoun, a believer in states' rights, came up with an idea to combat the tariffs. He said that any state could declare a federal law invalid if the state did not agree with it. Calhoun's idea, called nullification, met with opposition from both the North and the South.

Even Davis disagreed with nullification as a solution to the issue of tariffs. When there was a chance that he would be transferred to South Carolina to enforce the collection of tariffs, Davis decided he would rather resign from the Army than march against South Carolina. Eventually, a compromise was reached. The tariff would be gradually lowered over a ten-year period. But the split between North and South widened.

JOHN C. CALHOUN SERVED AS THE SEVENTH
VICE PRESIDENT OF THE UNITED STATES
FROM 1825 TO 1832.
HE WAS A STRONG SUPPORTER OF SLAVERY.

★

17

COMPROMISE OF 1850

The rapid westward expansion reopened old wounds as far as whether new territories should be free or slave states. When the United States **annexed** Texas in 1845, this led to the Mexican-American War, fought between 1846 and 1848.

All the new land the U.S. had won needed to be incorporated into the Union. The delicate balance between slave state and free state was all that was keeping the Union free from outright bloodshed between the two impassioned **factions**.

In this image, the texas flag flies over the Alamo in San Antonio. Texas became a state in December 1845.

OREGON
TERRITORY

UTAH
TERRITORY

UNORGANIZED
TERRITORY

CA
1850

NEW MEXICO
TERRITORY

TX
1845

FREE STATES AND TERRITORIES

SLAVE STATES AND TERRITORIES

OPEN TO SLAVERY BY THE COMPROMISE OF 1850

MISSOURI COMPROMISE LINE

To stave off violence, Henry Clay proposed the Compromise of 1850. The compromise consisted of five main points. California would be admitted to the Union as a free state. Utah and New Mexico territories would be able to decide for themselves whether to allow slavery. Texas's boundaries were set at their present place and they had to relinquish claims to the other lands that were part of the state after the war. The fourth part of the compromise abolished the slave trade in Washington, D.C. (but did not abolish slavery there), and finally the Fugitive Slave Act was strengthened. Both sides were somewhat satisfied with the compromise and it put off any violence until 1854.

HENRY CLAY

BLEEDING KANSAS

As more Americans moved west, more territories sought to become states. When the vast area west of Iowa and Missouri wanted to join the Union, a law was passed splitting it into two states, Kansas and Nebraska. But would these states be slave or free? Since they were above the Missouri Compromise line, which required new states to be free, it seemed that the matter was settled. But the law created in 1854, called the Kansas-Nebraska Act, stated that the people living in those states should decide the question of slavery. Northern states were outraged, for this voided the Missouri Compromise. Soon the race was on for control of the new states. The phrase "bleeding Kansas" began to describe the terrible bloodshed that exploded as proslavery and antislavery groups clashed.

FREE STATES AND TERRITORIES

SLAVE STATES AND TERRITORIES

OPEN TO SLAVERY BY THE COMPROMISE OF 1850

OPEN TO SLAVERY BY KANSAS-NEBRASKA ACT, 1854

MISSOURI COMPROMISE LINE

THE KANSAS-NEBRASKA ACT OF 1854
WAS DRAFTED BY PRESIDENT FRANKLIN PIERCE
AND SENATOR STEPHEN DOUGLAS OF ILLINOIS.

CIVIL WAR

The South saw its way of life slipping away. The election of Abraham Lincoln as president in 1860 was the final blow. By February 1861, seven Southern states had **seceded** from the Union, and Davis had been chosen president of the Confederacy. Davis did not want to see the United States split apart. He even sent a peace commission to Washington, D.C., to try to prevent war. But the rift between North and South had grown too large.

On February 18, 1861, a band played "Dixie" as Davis mounted the steps of the state capitol in Montgomery, Alabama, to give his inaugural address. He concluded his speech by saying, "We may hopefully look forward to success, to peace, and to prosperity." Despite these stirring words, however, the next four years would spell the end of all three for Davis and the new nation he led.

THE AMERICAN CIVIL WAR BEGAN IN 1861.
BY THE TIME IT ENDED IN 1865, MANY BLOODY
BATTLES HAD BEEN FOUGHT BETWEEN NORTH
AND SOUTH, AND MANY LIVES HAD BEEN LOST.

WHOSE RIGHTS ARE THEY ANYWAY?

The Tenth Amendment to the U.S. Constitution states that "The powers not delegated to the United States by the Constitution, nor prohibited by it to the States, are reserved to the States respectively, or to the people." That is a formal way of saying that the individual states have the right to do anything not specifically granted to the federal government by the Constitution.

It does seem rather simple. With this amendment, the Founding Fathers intended to protect American citizens from a too-powerful federal government. But over the years, some people interpreted the Tenth Amendment to suit their own purposes.

THE BILL OF RIGHTS, RATIFIED IN 1791,
WAS COMPRISED OF
THE FIRST TEN AMENDMENTS
TO THE U.S. CONSTITUTION.

John C. Calhoun was a Democrat from South Carolina and vice president under presidents John Quincy Adams and Andrew Jackson. Early in his political career, Calhoun favored national interests over those of the individual states. But by 1828, he had become angry about the effect of tariffs on the economy of his home state. Making a complete turnaround, Calhoun began promoting the rights of the states over those of the federal government. His doctrine of nullification said that a state could ignore a federal law with which it disagreed. Taken to its extreme conclusion, nullification implied that a state could even leave the Union if its differences with the national government became too great.

The argument for states' rights led to the secession of the Southern states in an effort to preserve their right to own slaves. And yet the new nation, the Confederate States of America, ultimately was doomed by the same claim. Using states' rights as their motto, many in the South refused to cooperate with President Jefferson Davis as he tried to form the individual Confederate states into a cohesive whole capable of fighting the Union army.

GLOSSARY

abolition: Getting rid of slavery.

annexed: Added.

compromises: Agreements to settle an argument where each side gives up a little of what they want.

economy: The wealth and resources of a country or region.

electoral college: A body of voters chosen to elect the president and vice president of the United States.

factions: Small, organized, dissenting groups within a larger one, usually political.

indentured: Bound by contract into service for another.

indivisible: Undividable or unable to be broken apart.

knell: The tolling of a bell signaling disaster.

plantation: An estate on which crops such as tobacco, sugar, and coffee are grown by resident workers.

precedent: An act or instance that is used as an example when dealing with similar circumstances at a later time.

prohibited: Not allowed; forbidden; banned.

seceded: Withdrew formally from membership in a federal union, an alliance, or a political or religious organization.

sectional: Relating to a particular district or area.

tariffs: Taxes or duties to be paid on certain imports or exports.

territory: An organized segment of a country that is not yet granted the full rights of a state.

FOR MORE INFORMATION

BOOKS

Hinton, KaaVonia. *To Preserve the Union: Causes and Effects of the Missouri Compromise.* Mankato, MN: Capstone Press, 2013.

Lanier, Wendy. *What Was the Missouri Compromise?: And Other Questions About the Struggle over Slavery.* New York: Lerner Publishing, 2012.

WEBSITES

The Compromise of 1850
http://www.ushistory.org/us/30d.asp

The Compromise of 1850 and the Fugitive Slave Act
https://www.pbs.org/wgbh/aia/part4/4p2951.html

INDEX